FIRST 50 SONGS

YOU SHOULD PLAY ON THE CELLO

ISBN 978-1-5400-7010-4

Visit Hal Leonard Online at
www.halleonard.com

Contact us:
Hal Leonard
7777 West Bluemound Road
Milwaukee, WI 53213
ail: info@halleonard.com

In Europe, contact:
Hal Leonard Europe Limited
42 Wigmore Street
Marylebone, London, W1U 2RN
Email: info@halleonardeurope.com

In Australia, contact:
Hal Leonard Australia Pty. Ltd.
4 Lentara Court
Cheltenham, Victoria, 3192 Australia
Email: info@halleonard.com.au

CONTENTS

AIR ON THE G STRING
from ORCHESTRAL SUITE NO. 3 IN D MAJOR, BWV 1068

CELLO

By JOHANN SEBASTIAN BACH

Slowly and expressively

ALL YOU NEED IS LOVE

CELLO

Words and Music by JOHN LENNON
and PAUL McCARTNEY

ALL OF ME

CELLO

Words and Music by JOHN STEPHENS
and TOBY GAD

Slowly, in 2

1st time D.C.
2nd time Fine

1.

2.

D.S. al Fine
(take 1st ending)

AMAZING GRACE

CELLO

Traditional American Melody

AVE MARIA
adapted from "Prelude in C Major" by Johann Sebastian Bach

By CHARLES GOUNOD

CELLO

BASIN STREET BLUES

CELLO

Words and Music by
SPENCER WILLIAMS

BEST SONG EVER

CELLO

Words and Music by EDWARD DREWETT,
WAYNE HECTOR, JULIAN BUNETTA
and JOHN RYAN

CARNIVAL OF VENICE

CELLO

By JULIUS BENEDICT

Moderately, with motion

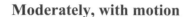

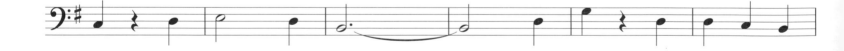

CIRCLE OF LIFE

from THE LION KING

Cello

Music by ELTON JOHN
Lyrics by TIM RICE

Moderately (with an African beat)

EVERMORE
from BEAUTY AND THE BEAST

CELLO

Music by ALAN MENKEN
Lyrics by TIM RICE

Sturdy Ballad

FLY ME TO THE MOON
(In Other Words)

Cello

Words and Music by
BART HOWARD

FIGHT SONG

CELLO

Words and Music by RACHEL PLATTEN
and DAVE BASSETT

THE FOOL ON THE HILL

CELLO

Words and Music by JOHN LENNON
and PAUL McCARTNEY

GOD BLESS AMERICA®

CELLO

Words and Music by
IRVING BERLIN

THE GODFATHER
(Love Theme)

from the Paramount Picture THE GODFATHER

CELLO

By NINO ROTA

HALLELUJAH

CELLO

Words and Music by
LEONARD COHEN

Moderately slow, in 2

HAPPY
from DESPICABLE ME 2

CELLO

Words and Music by
PHARRELL WILLIAMS

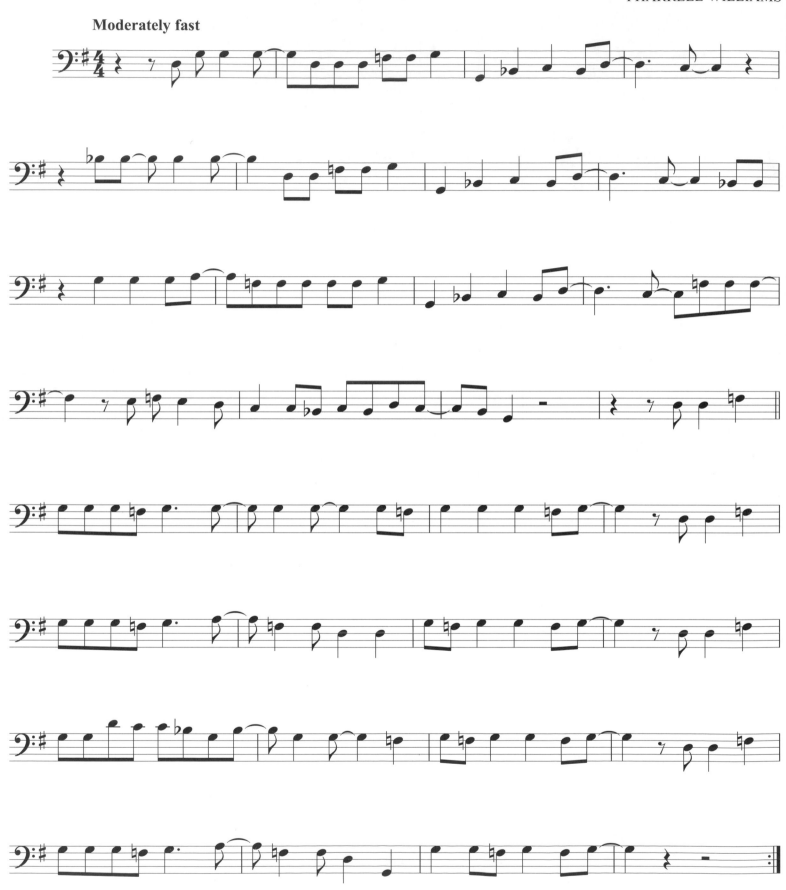

HELLO

CELLO

Words and Music by
LIONEL RICHIE

Slow Ballad

HELLO, DOLLY!

from HELLO, DOLLY!

CELLO

Music and Lyric by
JERRY HERMAN

HOW DEEP IS YOUR LOVE

from the Motion Picture SATURDAY NIGHT FEVER

CELLO

Words and Music by BARRY GIBB,
ROBIN GIBB and MAURICE GIBB

THE HUSTLE

CELLO

Words and Music by
VAN McCOY

I WILL ALWAYS LOVE YOU

featured in THE BODYGUARD

CELLO

Words and Music by
DOLLY PARTON

Moderately slow

JUST GIVE ME A REASON

CELLO

Words and Music by ALECIA MOORE,
JEFF BHASKER and NATE RUESS

CODA

JUST THE WAY YOU ARE

CELLO

Words and Music by BRUNO MARS,
ARI LEVINE, PHILIP LAWRENCE,
KHARI CAIN and KHALIL WALTON

Moderately

To Coda ⊕

Fine

D.S. al Coda

CODA ⊕

D.S. al Fine

LET IT GO
from FROZEN

CELLO

Music and Lyrics by KRISTEN ANDERSON-LOPEZ
and ROBERT LOPEZ

Slowly, in 2

MAS QUE NADA

CELLO

Words and Music by
JORGE BEN

MY HEART WILL GO ON

(Love Theme from 'Titanic')

from the Paramount and Twentieth Century Fox Motion Picture TITANIC

CELLO

Music by JAMES HORNER
Lyric by WILL JENNINGS

NATURAL

Cello

Words and Music by DAN REYNOLDS,
WAYNE SERMON, BEN McKEE,
DANIEL PLATZMAN, JUSTIN TRANTOR,
MATTIAS LARSSON and ROBIN FREDRICKSSON

THE PLACE WHERE LOST THINGS GO

from MARY POPPINS RETURNS

CELLO

Music by MARC SHAIMAN
Lyrics by SCOTT WITTMAN and MARC SHAIMAN

NIGHT TRAIN

CELLO

Words by OSCAR WASHINGTON
and LEWIS C. SIMPKINS
Music by JIMMY FORREST

PURE IMAGINATION

from WILLY WONKA AND THE CHOCOLATE FACTORY

CELLO

Words and Music by LESLIE BRICUSSE
and ANTHONY NEWLEY

ROAR

Cello

Words and Music by KATY PERRY,
MAX MARTIN, DR. LUKE,
BONNIE McKEE and HENRY WALTER

ROLLING IN THE DEEP

CELLO

Words and Music by ADELE ADKINS
and PAUL EPWORTH

SATIN DOLL

CELLO

By DUKE ELLINGTON

SEE YOU AGAIN
from FURIOUS 7

Cello

Words and Music by CAMERON THOMAZ,
CHARLIE PUTH, JUSTIN FRANKS,
ANDREW CEDAR, DANN HUME,
JOSH HARDY and PHOEBE COCKBURN

SHAKE IT OFF

CELLO

Words and Music by TAYLOR SWIFT,
MAX MARTIN and SHELLBACK

SHALLOW
from A STAR IS BORN

CELLO

Words and Music by STEFANI GERMANOTTA,
MARK RONSON, ANDREW WYATT
and ANTHONY ROSSOMANDO

Moderately

STAND BY ME

CELLO

Words and Music by JERRY LEIBER,
MIKE STOLLER and BEN E. KING

Moderately, with a beat

THE STAR-SPANGLED BANNER

CELLO

Words by FRANCIS SCOTT KEY
Music by JOHN STAFFORD SMITH

50

STAY WITH ME

CELLO

Words and Music by SAM SMITH,
JAMES NAPIER, WILLIAM EDWARD PHILLIPS,
TOM PETTY and JEFF LYNNE

STOMPIN' AT THE SAVOY

Cello

By BENNY GOODMAN,
EDGAR SAMPSON and CHICK WEBB

SUMMERTIME

from PORGY AND BESS®

CELLO

Music and Lyrics by GEORGE GERSHWIN,
DuBOSE and DOROTHY HEYWARD
and IRA GERSHWIN

THE SWAN
(Le cygne)
from CARNIVAL OF THE ANIMALS

CELLO

By CAMILLE SAINT-SAËNS

Slowly, with expression

Optional 8va all

TEQUILA

CELLO

By CHUCK RIO

THIS IS ME

from THE GREATEST SHOWMAN

CELLO

Words and Music by BENJ PASEK
and JUSTIN PAUL

UPTOWN FUNK

CELLO

Words and Music by MARK RONSON,
BRUNO MARS, PHILIP LAWRENCE, JEFF BHASKER, DEVON GALLASPY,
NICHOLAUS WILLIAMS, LONNIE SIMMONS, RONNIE WILSON,
CHARLES WILSON, RUDOLPH TAYLOR and ROBERT WILSON

Moderately

VIVA LA VIDA

CELLO

Words and Music by GUY BERRYMAN,
JON BUCKLAND, WILL CHAMPION
and CHRIS MARTIN

WHAT A WONDERFUL WORLD

Cello

Words and Music by GEORGE DAVID WEISS
and BOB THIELE

WHAT ABOUT US

CELLO

Words and Music by ALECIA MOORE,
STEVE MAC and JOHNNY McDAID

YOU'RE MY BEST FRIEND

CELLO

Words and Music by
JOHN DEACON